THE GOOD ROAD

THE GOOD ROAD
published by Multnomah Books
a part of the Questar Publishing family

© 1997 by Janet Paschal

International Standard Book Number: 1-57673-137-5

Design by D2 DesignWorks/David Carlson
Photography by Tamara Reynolds

Printed in the USA

Scripture quotes are from:
The Holy Bible, New International Version (NIV)
© 1973, 1984 by International Bible Society,
used by permission of Zondervan Publishing House

The New King James Version (NKJV)
© 1984 by Thomas Nelson, Inc.

The King James Version (KJV)

For information:
Questar Publishers, Inc.
Post Office Box 1720
Sisters, Oregon 97759

Paschal, Janet.
    The good road: a book about my journey with God and the people
He used to touch my life / Janet Paschal.
        p.   cm.
    ISBN 1-57673-137-5 (alk. paper)
    1. Paschal, Janet. 2. Christian biography—United States. 3. Christian life. I. Title
BR1725.P266A3 1997
277.3'082'092—dc21
                                    96-48099
                                    CIP

97 98 99 00 01 02 03 — 10 9 8 7 6 5 4 3 2 1

THE GOOD ROAD

Encounters Along the Way

JANET PASCHAL

PHOTOGRAPHY BY TAMARA REYNOLDS

MULTNOMAH BOOKS ❧ SISTERS, OREGON

Contents

Set up signposts, Make landmarks; Set your heart toward the highway...." Jeremiah 31:21 NKJV ❧ We are called to undertake a lifetime pilgrimage; to follow a trail broadened by those before us. God directs us to construct road signs, powerful reminders of His unwavering faithfulness, knowing they will propel us and those who follow along the good road. ❧ We all take different roads home. Each of us is heading for the same destination, but we face our own variety of twists and turns and narrow places, as well as a few stretches that are all downhill. ❧ You and I encounter differing relationships, experiences and challenges, only to realize that somewhere along the way we arrive at the same impasse. It is a threshold to be weighed and pondered. A directive to be decided. A summons that will change our past, present and future. ❧ It is a holy whisper, "Follow Me." —Janet Paschal

Part One

The Way of Trust

I have deliberated endless theologies.

I have questioned "Why?" and "Why not?" I have gazed at the stars on a clear night and asked, "Are You really there?" There is a place in Christ where simple trust replaces tangibles, emotion and reason.

The Road Ahead

It was a night of celebration. Twenty-four thousand people gathered in Charlotte, North Carolina, to usher in a new year and pay tribute to the old. We sang, worshipped and celebrated the belief that we'd find Christ involved in the upcoming days and seasons of our lives.

Amid crowded hallways and perpetual lines, a gentleman shook my hand and said very quietly, "I'd like to ask you to pray for me. I pastor a large church nearby and I've just been diagnosed with cancer."

While I was weighing options for my future, this pastor was fighting for his.

Standing on the threshold of a new year makes me think ahead to expectations and inevitable surprises. What dreams will God intercept, improve upon and make reality? What homes will He heal and restore? What imperfect vessels will He touch with the gifts of writing, humor or speaking?

What giants will rise up? What unseemly heroes will march out to challenge them? Will there will be born another John Wesley, John Bunyan or Mother Teresa? Will there emerge world peace or a remedy for famine?

Will people I love be handed lab results that read "incurable" or "malignant"? Does death wait for any of us, eager to dance its mournful rhythm?

Whatever secrets a new year holds, we will never encounter them alone. There will always be at least two to plow through the tragedies and graciously take the bows. There'll be two to lead the choir and visit the alcoholic. Two to uproot complacency and awaken compassion. Two. Sometimes more, but never less. Christ and you. Christ and me.

We do not wonder if the weeks ahead will surprise or overwhelm Him. We do not wonder whether He will walk into our emergency rooms and cancer centers. We do not wonder if He is acquainted with grief or familiar with sorrow.

We'll follow Him over the grassy knolls of a family cemetery. We'll lean in to hear His voice amid the heart-wrenching sound of grief.

We question His plans, but not His faithfulness. We pause at His ways, but not His wisdom. We wonder what a new year holds, but we never wonder Who holds it.

"For I know the plans I have for you," declares the LORD, "plans to prosper you and not to harm you, plans to give you hope and a future." Jeremiah 29:11 NIV

I know I don't surprise You
You've known me from the start
My failures and successes
Well, Lord, You've seen them all
With all my resolutions
Still I stumble now and then
But You remain just like You've always been

Faithful, unchangeable
Ever present help when I'm in need
Counsellor, Lord You are wonderful
Patient, loving Father to me
In a world lost in uncertainties
I am sure You'll always be
An ever faithful Father
An ever faithful Father to me

And like a child who reaches
For things best left alone
And learns too late the Father
Really knew best all along
You held my hand in sorrow
You helped me to believe
You gently promised You would always be

JANET PASCHAL

Work In Progress

chapter Two

We were in search of it for its architecture and posterity. On this Ash Wednesday we walked to Christ Church, down-town Nassau, Bahamas.

Nassau boasts rare tropical flowers, exotic birds and lush, green gardens. One quick stroll along the palm-lined streets leaves you with the feeling God made this spot special. Standing tall amid the bustling streets is a temple — a refuge of sorts where, on this day, open windows ushered peaceful breezes into the sanctuary filled with sweet-smelling blossoms, archaic hymnals and sincere hearts.

Just as Mass was about to begin, my friends and I slipped into a polished, worn pew amid well-dressed Bahamians. The huge pipe organ began its solemn refrain. The congregation sang as if this were its lifeline. The bishop delivered the message and ladies and gentlemen lined up to receive communion. These believers were different from us in many ways, but intimately the same when we ate and drank in remembrance of Him.

The following year I returned to Nassau, anticipating an afternoon in that quiet refuge where I'd so profoundly sensed God the year before. I journeyed past vendors and other tourists, my heart filled with emotion and pent-up frustration. Christ Church was just as I remembered; architecturally sound but in need of paint and mortar maintenance. It didn't matter to me. I had a heart full of unresolved issues to pour out to God so the broken building seemed fitting, in a way.

I walked through huge doors into the sanctuary

and slipped into a pew. From overhead I heard voices and heavy feet followed by hammers and overseers barking orders. They were remodeling the balcony. My long-anticipated haven had become a bustling thoroughfare of carpenters, electricians and bricklayers. I couldn't believe it. Why did they have to be here today? Hadn't God known how much I needed this?

I silently ranted on. Finally it hit me. This is exactly what the church is for. Christ built His church so that men and women and teenagers and children could come and hammer out their salvation they received by grace. He compels people to come and piece together dreams that life may have dismantled. He bids us tear down old walls and build up new tomorrows. He calls us to reassess the strength of our foundation.

Construction in progress is never convenient. It is intrusive. It interrupts us. It strips us. It lays bare our weaknesses and vulnerability.

But who better to heal us than the Great Physician? Who better to understand our brokenness than the Man of Sorrows? Who better to reconstruct us than the Master Carpenter?

I walked away embarrassed I'd been so concerned with my own needs. God wanted to shift my focus away from my tiny arena and toward His more enduring objectives. My attitude had been in need of repair and, as usual, God knew just what was needed.

We have a building from God, an eternal house in heaven, not built by human hands. Meanwhile we groan, longing to be clothed with our heavenly dwelling.

2 Corinthians 5:1, 2 NIV

His Truth Keeps Marching On

They said it wouldn't last
Said God's word would pass into mere history
They thought the church He built would end
Replaced by modern times and trends
But generations keep reminding them

His truth keeps on marching, marching on
On a million Sunday mornings in a million little towns
Through a hungry little village in a foreign, distant land
And in the pew when someone stands to testify again
His truth keeps marching
His truth keeps marching on

So many kingdoms fall
Some give their all but build on sinking sand
While through the years God's church has grown
The solid rock, laid stone by stone
The kingdom that is built on Christ alone

Throughout the ages time has shown
When other gods have come and gone . . .

JANET PASCHAL

Detours

I was on an airplane answering mail while en route to Detroit. I pulled her letter from my seemingly regenerative stack and began to read.

"Dear Janet, I don't know if you'll remember me or not...."

Three years ago she'd written, "My husband of fifteen years walked in the door a few weeks ago, looked at me and said, 'I love you but I'm not sure I'm in love with you. I don't know if I want this marriage to continue.' We have two young daughters and in that one evening our worlds were completely turned upside down. I don't know what God will do in this situation but there is a song on your tape that I listen to every night. God has used it to remind me that He will be faithful 'Through Every Storm.' I just thought I'd let you know."

I remembered her. She'd written with a clarity that made me know her pain went deeper than her words ever could. I'd sent her some books, prayed for her occasionally and wondered how she was. Now, 30,000 feet over Michigan and three years later, I was about to find out.

She wrote that those years had been the most difficult of her life. There'd been mornings when there seemed little reason to face another day. There were days she'd wanted to give up completely. But God had other plans. Through an unusual set of circumstances her husband had surrendered his life to Christ. He was a changed man; active in church, growing in the Word, singing in the choir. She said both daughters had come to her individually and said, "Dad is so different now." She ended her letter, "For the first time in our lives, I have a husband and our girls have a father. I just thought I'd let you know."

I carefully folded the letter together, looked out the window of the American Airlines jetliner and whispered, "Well God, You came through again." It probably didn't happen the way she expected and I'm sure it wasn't according to her timetable, but in His own sovereign way, God rewrote the ending to her story. He parted another sea and moved another mountain. He took a thread of faith and stretched it out over three years and four hearts and one home. He penned another mystery while a company of angels looked on.

I have, on occasion, perceived God as indifferent. I've questioned why other situations didn't have happy endings. I've tiptoed beside the den of self-pity waiting for the tangible, the visible, then cast my fragile faith aside and crawled right in. But more often I've stood staring at closed doors, unaware that He was, even then, opening better ones.

He is a God of surprises and an orchestrator of impeccable timing. Just when we're ready to resign ourselves to a journey that stops short of signs and wonders He makes the most unexpected things happen: a change of heart, a change of perspective or, in some cases, a letter where you sense God saying, "I just thought I'd let you know."

I will restore to you the years the locusts have eaten . . . . Joel 2:25 KJV

GOD WILL MAKE A WAY

Must have felt strange to end up stranded between an army and a sea
They must have felt forsaken wondering why God wasn't all He said He'd be
When your back's against the wall
It's the hardest place of all
But somewhere between provision and impossibility

God will make a way
When there seems to be no way
Forever He is faithful
He will make a road
When you bear a heavy load
I know, God will make a way

When a wall of circumstances leaves you crying in the night
And you struggle 'til your strength is almost gone
God will gently hold you in the shelter of His heart
And carve a road for you to carry on
So carry on

JANET PASCHAL

Crossroads

chapter *Four*

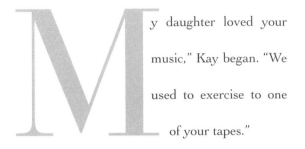y daughter loved your music," Kay began. "We used to exercise to one of your tapes."

Shannon, her daughter, was thirteen when she boarded a church bus after a day with her youth group at an amusement park. Around eleven o'clock that evening, a drunken driver crossed the median and hit the bus head-on. It exploded into flames. Shannon and twenty-three other young people perished.

Shannon would never reach her fourteenth birthday. She would never wear the new clothes she'd painstakingly arranged on her bed. She'd never graduate or drive a car or fall in love.

Now, nine years later, Kay sits across the table from me and says, "I thought I would never laugh again. We were so close, it was as though a part of me died." She continued, "Her father and I eventually moved to another state to escape the memories."

"Did you ever ask God why?" I ask.

She smiled. "I had to reassess everything I knew about Christ. I knew Shannon had surrendered her life to Him at a young age, but I kept thinking how much more I needed her than He did. I hurt for all the things she would miss in life. It changed me. I'm not the same person. I've resigned the accident to God's sovereignty, but some days, yes, I still wonder why."

I envy Kay's resolve. She spoke matter-of-factly, with a strength that only suffering can forge. She possessed a certain presence, as one who has learned important life lessons and need prove nothing.

I realized the strength which sustained Kay was not something God showered on her following the tragedy. It was an obstinate faith established through the years she had walked with Christ. It was the same gritty determination David must have felt when he encountered the looming giant—a deep knowledge that the God who had been faithful in the past would again prove Himself.

I sat thinking how closely she walked with Christ, but how overwhelming the price. Kay has discovered a place in Him where only suffering takes you—a depth of certainty that some never know. Little by little she has forfeited Shannon to God's custody.

Kay walks in places I have not been. She communes with Christ as only the truly broken can. She reminds me that we know Christ in the power of His resurrection, but we learn Him in the fellowship of His suffering. Lessons we do not soon forget. Miles of the journey that change us. Junctions in the road that make us all He intended.

My righteousness I hold fast, and will not let it go.

Job 27:6 NKJV

I have found a friend in Jesus
Like no other friend I've known
When I walk through desert places
I don't ever walk alone
He's a mountain, He's a shelter
In the corner He's a stone
He's the cleft within the rock
He is God and God alone

When the clouds above me threaten
And my spirit's feelin' low
When I'm barely holding steady
And the wind begins to blow
He's a strong and mighty refuge
The solid Rock I run to
With open arms He'll welcome me in
Rock of Ages, hide me again
O, Rock of Ages, hide me again

In the shelter of His keeping
In the shadow of His wings
Is a table spread with plenty
And I feast on His good things
He showers me with blessings
Then He draws me to His side
I don't fear the storm
When there's a peaceful place to hide

JANET PASCHAL/JOEL LINDSEY

Travelers' Junction

chapter *Five*

They had come from near and far, valiantly fighting holiday traffic, intense heat and crowded everything. For an entire weekend the new arena cozily nestled in the heart of the little resort town was filled to capacity for a musical celebration of Christ.

On the final evening I turned to leave the stage area and found myself behind a throng of people moving toward the main exit. Because they moved slowly, I struck out through the rows of seats and headed for the side door.

Midway between the rows it hit me. This is where the people sat. This was the audience vantage point for what we performers did on the platform.

I slid into one of the chairs and noticed the cramped leg room. I wondered where the ladies put their purses. It would have been difficult for someone in the middle of the row to leave during the concert. It might have been uncomfortable sitting that close to someone you didn't know.

For the artists, it was different. We'd had a hospitality room at our disposal. Our seats were the best in the house. We were being paid to be there. We'd been reaffirmed by audience reaction. Every night many sought us out to pay their own personal tributes, timid in their approach as though we had arrived at some special place they were yet to reach. Now I sat in the middle of the row thinking how they were probably miles ahead of me in the pursuit to be more like Christ.

All of a sudden I realized why I'd stopped and suddenly forgotten my own agenda while maneuvering between the rows: in reality, I had become comfortable taking more than I gave. I was supposed to be the servant, but the ladies and gentlemen in the audience were the real servants.

The hundreds occupying those seats were more than numbers compiling ticket and product sales. These were people who may have sacrificed much to be a part of our weekend. Who knew what challenges some would face when they returned home? Who knew how many had come trying to find answers for crucial questions or how many couples came praying that the weekend would have a positive influence on their relationships? How many came whose faith had suffered a crushing blow and who needed to be reminded that Jesus is still the greatest reality of all?

John the Baptist described his first encounter with Christ, saying, "I did not recognize Him . . ." (John 1:31, 33). God incarnate didn't stand out in the crowd. The longed-for Redeemer walked city streets without fanfare. The Alpha and Omega once again proved to be the *in-between* when humanity could not rise above itself.

One gets the feeling that Jesus would have chosen a seat midway between the rows.

Do not think of yourself more highly than you ought, but rather think of yourself with sober judgment.
Romans 12:3 NIV

I dusted off the mantle
And polished my good deeds
So proud the Master Builder chose
To come and live with me
Perhaps He'd add a window
Or a place where wishes go
I was planning bright tomorrows
When I felt the hammer's blow

He took a heart and built a home
Carved a place for perfect love to dwell
He made a room for Him alone
Following plans He knew so well
He tore apart a house of stone
Then took a heart and built a home

I raised the welcome banner
But I hoped He wouldn't see
The places I'd neglected
Deep inside of me
He walked through every chamber
Rooms of doubt and compromise
But when He raised the hammer
There was mercy in His eyes

He tore down weak foundations
Walls of fear and halls of gloom
He narrowed every comfort zone
To give His love some room

JANET PASCHAL

Part Two

When words fail to express the

depth of our gratitude, joy or

sorrow, the heart responds with

an understanding all its own.

The Winding Road

Lane Ends

chapter *Six*

I was in the Kansas City airport waiting for my flight home when a family sat in the gate area near me. There were five of them — a small boy and girl, their mother and grandparents. The children were going to visit their father for the summer, they told me, fulfilling the terms of the new custody agreement. This would be their first summer away.

I watched as the mother cleverly turned away from adjusting the children's sweaters and backpacks just in time to intercept her own persistent tears. Their grandfather, who appeared rugged and hard-working, occasionally lifted a callused hand to discreetly brush his cheek. The grandmother was the strong one, stubbornly willing herself to smile and maintain some degree of normalcy through this very extraordinary pain.

It always gets to me. Hearts divided. Lives severed. Love unresolved. Children made to live beyond their years by circumstances they did not create. Open wounds. Closed chapters. Divided loyalties. It is no wonder it hurts so much.

One of life's certainties is that it never stays the same. Change comes. People move in and out of our lives. Children become parents, and parents children. We change jobs, cities and long-distance carriers. Life turns a page and we encounter exciting beginnings; another page and we're forced to watch a chapter end. The plot becomes painful and we long to rewrite our stories. Endings are unexpected, unwelcome and sometimes irreconcilable.

Jesus knew there would be stretches of our journey when nothing made sense. He knew lanes would end without warning. He knew life would often demand that we drink from sorrow's cup — one healthy dose after another.

He knew the paralyzing loneliness of unwanted endings. He knew the pain of denial by someone He loved and the sorrow of deception by someone He chose. He knew the feeling of abandonment by the very One who sent Him.

It is a good thing that "...we have not an high priest which cannot be touched with the feeling of our infirmities..." (Hebrews 4:15 KJV). It is a good thing that Jesus was "...a man of sorrows, and acquainted with grief..." (Isaiah 53:3 KJV). It is good that He understands just how painful endings can be.

When you pass through the waters, I will be with you; and when you pass through the rivers, they will not sweep over you. When you walk through the fire, you will not be burned; the flames will not set you ablaze.

Isaiah 43:2 NIV

Life deals from the bottom
The winner takes the day
Survival of the fittest
I think they say
Yet all the while we chase our dreams
Deep in our hearts we know
To win and lose is just the way life goes

(But) Love goes wherever a heart is breaking
And love runs to lighten a heavy load
And love shows mercy to all who will take it
Love came to let us know
That always, that's the way love goes

When faced with disappointment
It's hard to understand
That somewhere in the scheme of things
God has a master plan
We try so hard to figure out
What Heaven only knows
But sometimes that's just the way life goes

Love doesn't wait for the answers
To life's unpredictable plays
'Cause love never needed a reason
To stay
God made love that way

JANET PASCHAL

Crowded Passages

chapter *Seven*

Calcutta awakens to a religious chant. I walk down to the river where every day hundreds wade into the water to bathe. A few yards away, some buy incense and flowers to adorn a god of stone that sits silent, unhearing. Others burn dead bodies while onlookers pray the reincarnated lives of these people will be better. Smoke rises to God's sky. Lambs are slaughtered and the blood applied to men's and women's faces and necks for penance.

Calcutta, India, is a city of thirteen million people who live in an area the size of the Dallas/Ft. Worth airport. Mission of Mercy* was birthed there forty years ago when a young missionary couple set up a tent revival and put down roots. Mark and Huldah Buntain have literally changed the tomorrows of thousands of thrown-away children.

The Mission of Mercy Boys' Home is filled to capacity with abandoned boys. Their need goes beyond a remedy for hunger. They need to be hugged, talked to, made to laugh. I keep thinking how important they are to God. Their hearts pump life because God formed man of dust, breathed into his nostrils the breath of life and called it good. These boys laugh and cry, feel pain and joy because God made them that way.

At the Blind Children's School, boys and girls stand shakily and somewhat out of sync. Their arm movements are erratic and their eyes scale the ceiling as though, at some time, a light might dawn. They are vulnerable and uncoordinated. But when they sing "Standing On The Promises", it is as though all the earth quiets to hear. When they help me sing "Amazing Grace", I kneel beside one fragile girl and touch her hands, her face, while she sings, "I was blind, but now I see...." At that moment I, too, see a little more clearly.

Never again will I remain unaffected by people like these. When I see a picture of a child standing in a food line, I am reminded of the time the children in Calcutta held their plastic bags for me to fill with rice. When I walk through a toy department I am reminded of the simple toys they made from sticks and rags. A summer breeze makes me remember the putrid smells they lived with daily and hardly noticed. I recall their fragile frames, swollen bellies and wide, dark eyes.

I used to wonder what would compel a person to leave the comforts and opportunities of our country to go to a land of disease and hopelessness. Now I know. I pray I will never forget.

Then the righteous will answer him, "Lord, when did we see you hungry and feed you, or thirsty and give you something to drink?" [He] will reply, "... whatever you did for one of the least of these ... you did for me."
Matthew 25:37, 40 NIV

*Mission of Mercy is a Christian organization dedicated to meeting the physical and spiritual needs of hurting people all over the world. For more information, call 1-800-864-0200 or write P.O. Box 62600, Colorado Springs, CO 80962

HOLD ON TO THE NIGHT

No one likes to cry
But life is just that way sometimes
We all live and die
We all feel the rain sometimes
When darkness comes, embrace it
A storm is what you make it

Hold on to the night
For strength is gained in sorrow
And He is never closer than when we hurt alone
Lay it at His feet
Surrender is so sweet
The morning's just in sight
But 'til you see the light
Hold on to the night

Handle it with care
Cover it with prayer
Don't waste a single moment there

JANET PASCHAL

Yield

chapter *Eight*

I was answering mail aboard a flight to Denver when I noticed a letter with familiar handwriting. This young woman has written to me for several years. She is a Native American single mother. Her English is poor, her spelling worse and her handwriting almost illegible. Yet she never allows my birthday or a holiday to pass without sending me a card and a recent picture of her son. Occasionally she includes an inexpensive but important gift. My favorite was a battery-operated, lighted rose — the only one I've ever seen.

I don't know why Maria writes. I don't know what I give her. My notes are brief, sometimes generic and never as frequent as hers. The few times she's called the office she never seemed to have a specific reason. At the end of our conversation the operator always came on the line reminding Maria that she must deposit an additional seventy-five cents to continue talking.

I think of Maria often. Every time I'm in the company of important people who are movers and shakers, she comes to mind. When I meet power brokers and political masters, I think of her vulnerability. When I meet families who cannot afford to buy my music, I think of how little they, like Maria, have but how much in spirit they are able to give. Maria's opinion will not matter to the person who determines my next record budget or schedules next year's concert itinerary, but her simplicity sheds light on my own complex needs.

God is the great equalizer. He warns us: "You say, 'I am rich: I have acquired wealth and do not need a thing.' But you do not realize that you are wretched, pitiful, poor, blind and naked. I counsel you to buy from me gold refined in the fire, so you can become rich; and white clothes to wear, so you can cover your shameful nakedness; and salve to put on your eyes, so you can see" (Revelation 3:17, 18 NIV).

Maria has helped me understand that behind the door of every low-rent housing project is a person with a unique story. In every homeless shelter lives someone with needs, goals and disillusionments just like mine.

Maria asks nothing of me, but I ask of her to help me see beyond myself, past my neighborhood and into the corner of the world where her heart beats and her dreams live. I ask her to help me grasp the fact that, to God, whether we live in tenements or penthouses, we all look just the same.

For the poor shall never cease out of the land: therefore I command thee, saying, Thou shalt open thine hand wide unto thy brother, to thy poor, and to thy needy, in thy land. Deuteronomy 15:11 KJV

I'm pressing on the upward way
New heights I'm gaining every day
Still praying as I'm onward bound
Lord, plant my feet on higher ground

My heart has no desire to stay
Where doubts arise and fears dismay
'Tho some may dwell where these abound
My prayer, my aim is higher ground

I want to live above the world
'Tho Satan's darts at me are hurled
For faith has sought the joyful sound
The song of saints on higher ground

I want to scale the utmost height
And catch a gleam of glory bright
But still I'll pray 'til heaven I've found
Lord, lead me on to higher ground

Lord, lift me up and let me stand
By faith on heaven's tableland
A higher plane than I have found
Lord, plant my feet on higher ground

JOHNSON OATMAN, JR.
P.D.

Dark Tunnels

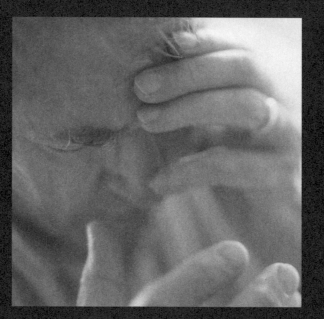

chapter *Nine*

I was singing for a service honoring the city's soldiers returning from war. The audience was visibly moved by the young men and women in uniform who lined the walls. The soldiers were tall and erect with a look of dignified humility. Church and civic leaders shook the hands of the honorees. Each was presented a plaque recognizing his or her unselfish service as the families glowed with unabashed pride — and rightly so.

The faces of one couple, however, reflected a different emotion. They were seated front and center as recipients of a special plaque. I had been told the father was not expected to come. "Too difficult," they'd said. His son was the city's only casualty of the Gulf War. The man's eyes were downcast. The couple's pain was deep. They frequently intercepted stray tears. Their pain had taken its toll on this family's countenance, stance and posture. Death had stolen more than their son.

I watched this couple as the ceremonies progressed. I wondered if we were imposing on their sorrow. Did they picture their son standing in line, receiving his honors? Did they wonder why it turned out this way? Did they ask God, "Why?" One soldier gave a tearful account of his rescue from enemy territory. He said he knew "God had performed a miracle." I wondered if the parents of the man who died felt God had been unfair. Had He chosen another man to live and their son to die?

I wanted the ceremonial speaker to say we do not understand things all the time. I wanted him to say one person doesn't live because he deserves to and another die because he doesn't. I wanted someone to say a lot of things happen without our understanding or approval, but nothing happens without God's knowledge.

I confess that in my lifetime I have repeatedly asked God, "Why?" I also admit that He has seldom responded. I conclude, therefore, that since He is God and I am merely one of His creations, He is not obligated to explain His often mysterious ways to me. But He has promised that He will sit up all night with us, catch every escaping tear and meticulously replace each fragile piece of shattered heart.

I will never leave you nor forsake you.

Hebrews 13:5 NKJV

SPRING WILL COME AGAIN

Like dawn her heart was breaking

She brushed away a tear

And looked out on the garden he had tended all those years

The chilling wind of winter

Had brought an early snow

But nothing matched the chill of loneliness she'd come to know

But very soon spring will come again

The sun will wake the morning, the loneliness will end

Hold on for the moment when

Night will pass and then

The birds will sing and spring will come again

As sure as sorrow passes

Winters quickly fade

And the Maker of the seasons grows a flowering parade

Then He paints another morning

On a canopy of snow

Knowing well the tears of winter make the springtime flowers grow

JANET PASCHAL

Paths Unknown

A single twenty-nine-year-old wrote to me, "I get so lonely. I want a husband to love me." She had my attention. I could relate. I could have erased her name and signed it with any number of names — including my own.

It is what all young (and not so young) girls dream of. Marriage is a union of indescribable reward, but with a high price tag. It calls for commitment. It requires selfless sacrifice. It responds to nothing less than complete abandon.

I am single. I have not stood among friends while the man of my idealistic dreams placed a ring on my finger symbolizing I was no longer the exclusive decision-maker for my life. Signifying that it mattered to someone else what happened in my world, my job, my day. Proclaiming someone else had long-term plans that included me in a big way.

I have not known the responsibility of nurturing a marriage relationship or what it means to have a husband and children require something of me. I have not known the joy of gazing into a giggly face while someone with my eyes or my jaw line smiled back. I have yet to look forward to growing old with someone.

I have seen marriages I envied and hoped the couple recognized the treasure they possessed. I've observed other marriages so painful that one or both people became gradually empty, despairing of life itself.

Countless people ask why I'm still single. Most often, they presume I have chosen to remain alone or they perceive my situation as a problem they can solve. They all mean well. But each, in his or her own way, lends to my sense of unfulfillment. They verify my fear that I may never get married. They unwittingly remind me that I should be married and have children on solid food. Without meaning to, they delegate me to that section of society that is not yet as broad or fulfilled as they.

As I change from one age bracket to the next, the qualities I'm looking for are changing. I've dated men with beautiful hearts and plain faces. I've observed selfishness in the well-conditioned and well-to-do. I've suspected one or two suitors may have embraced Christianity because of my commitment, not theirs. I just want them to be who they are.

I know my first priority is the pursuit of Christ. I know I am the apple of His eye. I know I am made whole and complete by intimate relationship with Him.

I don't know whether God has marriage in His plans for me. I sure hope so. But I'm accepting the reality that life is too short to compromise my walk with Him for anything other than what He deems best. On good days, I grasp it. On bad days, I remind myself that He is always up to something. I need only wait and watch it unfold.

...I have loved thee with an everlasting love....
Jeremiah 31:3 KJV

If I'd had my way about it
I'd have danced in grassy fields and fragrant meadows
And risen in the morning just to hear the robin's lovely melody
I'd have rested in wide spaces, high above the hurting places
And found a cross that asked much less of me
Never sailed in raging wind or troubled sea
If You'd thought it best to leave it up to me

But if I'd had my way
I might have been wading through the river
When You wanted me to walk upon the sea
And if I'd had my say and all of my wants and whims and wishes
You knew how weak and shallow I would be
If I'd had my way

If I'd had my way about it
I'd have only known Your majesty and glory
And passed the cup of sorrow to somebody else more willing to receive
I'd have written lovely phrases, inspiring lofty praises
And soared above my own humanity
Wounded wouldn't die, hearts wouldn't bleed
If all along You'd left it up to me

. . . I trust Your wisdom over mine 'cause You've proven over time
That in my narrow way of seeing things I leave the best behind sometimes
I might not have stayed as close if I'd had my way

JANET PASCHAL

Part Three

I conclude that, for me, there is no

other way but to walk with Christ —

to study Him, to pursue Him. He has

carved a place in my heart that

yearns for Him. He constrains me, He

woos me. He calls me to follow Him.

The Journey of Grace

Children At Play

chapter *Eleven*

It was the last night of a concert tour in New England. I looked forward to a dash back to the lobby to settle into a comfortable chair when the evening was over. But when the final song ended, a line of people formed from the platform as far as I could see. Still, I was glad to talk to each one, for their stories were always better than mine.

Finally, the second to the last stepped up and said, "Tonight you've re-acquainted me with the God of my youth." She went on to say the children's portion of the concert had especially touched her. We'd sung songs she learned as a child in church. Since childhood she'd built a life centered on materialism and self-gratification. She'd left God in the Sunday School class along with a host of other needs she'd outgrown.

But tonight, she said, had brought it all back.

Feelings arose in me that I wanted to save for later — when I'd have time to dwell on them. I was haunted by a simple phrase "the God of my youth." God without question. God without having to understand or perceive or grasp Him. Simple faith. Simple trust. Extraordinary God.

I thought about another night, another concert when I'd asked a group of children what they knew about the story of Jonah and the whale. A bubbly, enthusiastic little girl raised her hand and said, "I know!" When I nodded to her, she shouted, "Free Willy!" Her ingenuous belief in God's word enabled her to put Jonah's whale into the same ocean as Disney's.

I remember when my faith was that simple. As a child, I sang about His love with unbridled enthusiasm. It never occurred to me to question His mysterious ways. This was God. I revered Him. I believed Him.

Jesus said unless we become like children we'll not enter His kingdom. Unless we accept some of the ironies of walking with Christ. Unless we believe in Someone we've never shared a meal with. Unless we grasp Jesus' example when little children were brought to Him: He stopped what He was doing, pulled them to Him and said the rest of us had a lot to learn from the least of these.

I'm still learning.

Except ye . . . become as little children, ye shall not enter into the kingdom of heaven. Matthew 18:3 KJV

THE LORD WILL GO BEFORE YOU

Are you standing in a narrow place not sure which way to go
Do you struggle with uncertainties and hold to things you know
In the dark abyss, remember this
Our God is there
You know He is
And it'll be all right, it will be all right
Children, it'll be all right

The Lord will go before you
And He whispers, "You don't have to be afraid"
The Lord will go before you
He will lead you to a quiet resting place
He will surround you, keep you night and day
The Lord will go before you, the Lord will go before you
The Lord will go before you all the way

He led Moses through the mighty deep
And shut old Pharaoh down
He toppled walls at Jericho
The seventh time around
In the lion's den He proved again
Although we don't know how or when
It'll be all right, it will be all right
Children, it'll be all right

JANET PASCHAL/JOEL LINDSEY

Summit Views

chapter *Twelve*

After what seems like a million landings at the Nashville airport, there are still only a few occasions when I've been able to spot the neighborhood and house I live in as my plane makes its final approach. My reaction is always the same. I'm surprised the yards look manicured, the trees lush and the streets well-planned.

Upon closer inspection, many of the yards could use a bag of fertilizer and a month of serious attention (not *my* yard, of course!). The lots are not perfectly rectangular by any means. Most of the trees would benefit from pruning. A fresh coat of paint wouldn't hurt any of the houses, including mine (no, make that *especially* mine).

It's all in one's perspective. A tired, old farmhouse looks like a Norman Rockwell creation when viewed from the window seat of a *747*. The towering expanse of the Grand Canyon can seem quite unextraordinary to a toddler who has yet to explore, unattended, the reaches of his own backyard. A despondent human being appears as a potential masterpiece when seen through the eyes of the Master.

Jesus chose to see the world through eyes of mercy. He shared a cup with one who would bow under pressure and deny Him, then christened him a "Rock." He broke bread with another who would moments later betray Him then weep bitterly because he loved Him still. He befriended those of questionable character and ill repute — not because He wanted to be different, but because He saw them differently. He saw what they could become and not just what they were.

He saw what they were meant to be.

If we could grasp Jesus' perspective, we would see our circumstances in a whole new light. If we would look through compassion's eyes we'd see each other for the first time. If we looked through His eyes, we'd better understand why He came here at all.

So we fix our eyes not on what is seen, but on what is unseen. 2 Corinthians 4:18 NIV

They packed their bags and packed their dreams
They left their home and left their things
Headed for a strange and distant land
Not understanding how or when or why God would have chosen them
They journeyed on and followed His command
And in a corner of the world and in the eyes of boys and girls
The light of hope began to shine again.

So take a cup of water
And break a piece of bread
Who, but God, can say how many thousands will be fed
The world looks, oh, so different
When seen through mercy's eyes

Light a candle in the dark
Bring hope to heavy hearts
Come and see the world the way He does

JANET PASCHAL

Historic Landmarks

chapter *Thirteen*

My grandfather was just released from the hospital again. Three major attacks have weakened his heart so it no longer adequately pumps fluids away. The doctors say it has simply worn out.

On my last visit to his home, I asked Grandpa to share, again, the story of his encounter with Christ. His eyes became wistful. He leaned his elbows on the kitchen table. He recounted how, during the Depression, a young evangelist held a gospel service nearby. For the first time, Grandpa heard the story of Christ. He recalled, "I was under such conviction of the Holy Spirit that I was miserable. Driving home I could think of nothing else. I lay awake, unable to sleep. Finally I prayed, 'Lord, if you'll let me live to go to church on Sunday morning, when the preacher gives the altar call, I'll be the first one down the aisle.'" That morning when the invitation was given, Grandpa walked away from drinking, gambling and a host of other transgressions. He never looked back.

Grandpa was the first one in my family courageous enough to take the Nazarene carpenter at His word; the first one daring enough to abandon everything else in order to gain Christ. He, too, was a carpenter. He built the little church that housed his evangelistic fire. More importantly, he built dreams and goals in the hearts of those of us who watched him drive nails and pour foundations. We watched our grandfather give selflessly when he had the least to give. We saw him work a full-time job and, at the same time, carve a tiny congregation out of our little town. He showed us the gospel day after day so it was only consequential that he preached it on Sundays.

I don't think Grandpa has ever been interviewed. He's won countless wars with little fanfare, but he's been laying up treasures where it really counts, where motives matter, where prayers prayed in secret are heralded for all to see. My grandparents say a night never passes when they don't both call every family member's name in prayer. Every night. Without fail. Only God knows where I would be were it not for those relentless prayers.

Grandpa's pace has slowed and his shoulders are no longer broad and strong. His back is not straight, nor his memory sharp. We know it's only a matter of time before he succumbs to the dying part of living. The doctors say he's already cheated death beyond their expectations. Those of us who know him think he's cheated Satan quite a few times, too: his life has spawned pastors, evangelists and one grateful Christian singer. He will leave behind an example of unbending faithfulness to God. We'll savor our memories of his fiery but friendly sermons and church services when he'd reach for his worn, slightly-out-of-tune guitar and sing, "Amazing Grace" or "Zion's Hill."

Grandpa always said, "In the long run, serving Christ will pay off." Now, half a century later, remembering him across the kitchen table, I'm realizing just how right he was.

But the mercy of the LORD is from everlasting to everlasting upon them that fear him, and his righteousness unto children's children. Psalm 103:17 KJV

ANOTHER SOLDIER'S COMING HOME

His back is bent and weary
His voice is tired and low
His sword is worn from battle
And his steps have gotten slow
But he used to walk on water
Or it seemed that way to me
I know he moved some mountains
And never left his knees

Strike up the band
Assemble the choir
Another soldier's coming home
Another warrior hears the call he's waited for so long
He'll battle no more
But he's won his wars
Make sure heaven's table has room for at least one more
Sing a welcome song
Another soldier's coming home

He faced the winds of sorrow
But his heart knew no retreat
He walked in narrow places
Knowing Christ knew no defeat
But now his steps turn homeward
So much closer to the prize
He's sounding kind of homesick
And there's a longing in his eyes

JANET PASCHAL

Rest Areas

chapter *Fourteen*

It was a Saturday night in Houston. I was on the fifth floor of the Omni Hotel in a room overlooking the gardens and pool area. When I settled in for the evening I decided to take advantage of the peaceful view. Sitting cross-legged on the floor in front of the huge window, I spent a few moments absorbing the beauty of the placid water and the manicured grounds. Then simply and quietly I began talking to God.

After some time passed, I noticed a lone traveler in the garden. He'd apparently taken the long route from the hotel's registration desk. He walked slowly, his tie loosened and his hair unkempt. A garment bag was flung over his shoulder. He carried a coat in one hand and an oversized briefcase in the other.

The man's shoulders sagged and his back bent, weary from the journey. He stopped and knelt by the pool, unburdened himself of his luggage, then slowly, deliberately ran his hand through the water. I could almost see him make up his mind to come back later. In a moment he picked up his bags and continued his trek to the little room that, for this night at least, he would call his own.

It was one of those times God tapped me on the shoulder to make sure I didn't miss the moment. One of those quiet invitations to share His perspective. It was God reminding me that we are all like the traveler.

Our journey is incomplete. We're strangers, trying to carve out a few comfortable places in a world that only tolerates us. Our load is heavy.

Some of the burdens are unnecessary — baggage we have ourselves brought along. We go busily to and fro armed with our laptops and diaper bags and good intentions. Our backs bend and our shoulders sag. Our gaits slow, our hearts break and our eyes cry. We wonder if He notices us on ordinary days.

We turn a corner and find ourselves in a place of refreshing. An oasis. A calm between storms. Maybe it is a phone call from an old friend. Maybe it is a hug for no reason. Always it is when we least expect it and most need it.

We journey on, resolved to follow Him at any cost. We plow through the storms knowing somewhere up ahead lies another peaceful garden and cool, soothing spring. We travel on knowing we will, someday, lay aside our burdens forever.

We continue because we long for the lasting place of rest He has prepared.

This is the rest wherewith ye may cause the weary to rest; and this is the refreshing. Isaiah 28: 12 KJV

When you see your aspirations
Turning to a distant dream
Praying that the road that rides from here to there
Is not as scary as it seems
If you're staring at tomorrow
Through a veil of past defeat
Just around the corner
Right around the bend
There are things you won't believe

Our God is up to something
Too high for you to know
Our God is up to something
He's always in control
Just like He said He would
Our God is up to something good

Best believe His hand will take you
To an unfamiliar place
And you might feel confounded
You may feel confused
By the mystery of His ways
That's the time to be reminded
That His providence is sure
And in every situation
Every circumstance
God is up to something good

No eye has seen
No ear has heard
The things that our Father has prepared . . .

JANET PASCHAL/JOEL LINDSEY/GEOFF THURMAN

Coming Home

It was a warm Saturday afternoon. A Carolina breeze was steadily moving through the long grass and the proud, full branches. I was driving home, back to the little corner of the world where I grew up. I was en route to a modest house on a corner lot bordered by pine trees, vegetable gardens and neighbors who still bake casseroles for each other.

I was thinking that when I arrive, my dad (most likely atop his newly painted tractor) will head across the freshly mown lawn. He'll hug me long and hard until the back door slams. My mom will reach for me, smiling, and announce, "I've a fresh pitcher of iced tea. Who's ready for a glass?" In a few moments my nephew will bound across the road, dog in tow.

I knew I'd spend the next few days with people who love me unconditionally. The number of records I sell doesn't matter to them. The awards I have or haven't received are insignificant. My career, whether rocketing or plummeting, is rarely mentioned. They just care that I come. They just want me.

What really matters is home. This is the stuff I am made of. This is what is important to me.

We are all on a homeward journey. God patiently plans our routes and polices our perils. He watches us maneuver through detours and treacherous places. He even sees us make an occasional wrong turn then keep going anyway.

But always He waits. Long ago He paved the way and marked the direction for us to come to Him. He prepared a place of rest that is beyond the reaches of our imaginations — a welcome center built by His own hand.

He doesn't care what religious label we bear. Our nationality or net worth won't matter. He just cares that we come. He just wants us home.

After my grandfather was diagnosed with Alzheimer's Disease he had trouble recognizing people and places, like his home. He kept insisting that it was someone else's house, and he wasn't home yet.

I guess he was right.

I go to prepare a place for you. John 14:2 KJV

DAUGHTER'S HEART

Dreams and lofty visions
I've gathered over time
Lots of far-off wishes
I keep inside
Towering ambitions
Things I've yet to do
Vie for my attention, too

But in this daughter's heart there'll always be room for You
A holy sanctuary
A place You call me to
There's been love I've won and lost
And love I just outgrew
But in this daughter's heart, no doubt about it
There'll always be a place for You

Soon, before you know it
The years will slip away
Leaving good intentions
Or so they say
I'll hold to things that matter
Take the better road
Other things will come and go

JANET PASCHAL

Good company in a journey makes the way seem the shorter.

IZAAK WALTON (1593-1683)

JANET PASCHAL   P.O. BOX 2568, BRENTWOOD, TN   37024-2568